Anthony Curcio's

# NBA ALL★STARS 2021

*Basketball Coloring Book*

THIS BOOK BELONGS TO:

Anthony Curcio's

# NBA ALL★STARS 2021

*Basketball Coloring Book*

## PLAYER POSITION

1 or 2 letters under players name that identifies their position.

**Basketball Terms:**
Some people just refer to each position by a number. These are the numbers assigned to each position.

| | | |
|---|---|---|
| 1 | PG | POINT GUARD |
| 2 | G | GUARD (shooting guard) |
| 3 | F | FORWARD (small forward) |
| 4 | PF | POWER FORWARD |
| 5 | C | CENTER |

## STATS KEY

**P**oints **P**er **G**ame    **R**ebounds **P**er **G**ame    **A**ssists **P**er **G**ame    **S**teals **P**er **G**ame

2018-19 Season Stats

| PPG | RPG | APG | SPG |
|---|---|---|---|
| 27.3 | 5.3 | 5.2 | 1.3 |

| FG% | FT% | 3PT% |
|---|---|---|
| 47.2 | 91.6 | 43.7 |

**F**ield **G**oal Percentage    **F**ree **T**hrow Percentage    **T**hree **P**pint Percentage

**RISING STAR**
This player has been in the NBA for 4 years or less.

# THE ALL★STARS

1

Stephen Curry

# 30

2018-19 Season Stats

| PPG | RPG | APG | SPG |
|-----|-----|-----|-----|
| 27.3 | 5.3 | 5.2 | 1.3 |

| FG% | FT% | 3PT% |
|-----|-----|------|
| 47.2 | 91.6 | 43.7 |

Stephen Curry was drafted by the Golden State Warriors in 2009 and since led them to three NBA Championships! Along the way, Steph also broke pretty much every 3-point record imaginable and became the first ever, unanimous MVP award winner. This means out of about 100 sports reporters/media who picked their top 5 in order 1-5, every single one listed 'Stephen Curry' at the top! Not bad for a guy who didn't receive a single D-1 college offer (and who also was 5'6" as a freshmen in high school!)

# 23

# LeBron JAMES
## PG/G/SF/PF

LOS ANGELES LAKERS

2018-19 Season Stats

| PPG | RPG | APG | SPG |
|-----|-----|-----|-----|
| 27.4 | 8.5 | 8.3 | 1.3 |

| FG% | FT% | 3PT% |
|-----|-----|------|
| 51.0 | 66.5 | 33.9 |

LeBron James, known by many as the greatest basketball player of all time, was born in Akron, Ohio in 1984 - which, we completely forgot to mention... did you know that Stephen Curry and LeBron James were born in the same city? What if we said, the same hospital too?! Yep! Baby LeBron was just a few years before Steph. Anyways, LeBron was the first overall pick in the 2003 NBA Draft, straight out of high school! He's pretty much done it all since, 3x NBA champion, 3x NBA Finals MVP, 4x NBA Most Valuable Player, 15x NBA All-Star Game... you know LeBron could have played receiver in the NFL too? The best of the best!

# 13

## JAMES
## HARDEN
### PG

### 2018-19 Season Stats

| PPG | RPG | APG | SPG |
|---|---|---|---|
| 36.1 | 6.6 | 7.5 | 2.0 |

| FG% | FT% | 3PT% |
|---|---|---|
| 44.2 | 87.9 | 36.8 |

HOUSTON ROCKETS

James Harden was born in 1989 in Los Angeles, California. After an amazing high school career, Harden went on to star at Arizona State University, where number 13 is retired by the team! NBA Sixth Man of the year, NBA Most Valuable Player, 7x NBA All-Star... And absolute scoring and stats machine. At point season ended in 19-20, Harden was averaging 34.4 ppg!

Joel Embiid

# 21

# JOEL EMBIID
## C

76ers

2018-19 Season Stats

| PPG | RPG | APG | SPG |
|------|------|------|------|
| 27.5 | 13.6 | 3.7 | 0.7 |

| FG% | FT% | 3PT% |
|------|------|------|
| 48.4 | 80.4 | 30.0 |

Joel Embiid, born in 1994 is from Cameroon and moved to the United States at age 16 to pursue his talent in basketball. Embiid was a five star recruit coming out of high school. Joel entered the 2014 NBA Draft after just one year of college hoops playing for Kansas. Since then... 2x NBA All-Star, 2x All-NBA Second Team, NBA All-Rookie First Team!

11

# IRVING
PG/G

NETS

2018-19 Season Stats

| PPG | RPG | APG | SPG |
|------|------|------|------|
| 23.8 | 5.0 | 6.9 | 1.5 |

| FG% | FT% | 3PT% |
|------|------|------|
| 48.7 | 87.3 | 40.1 |

Kyrie Irving (b. 1992) accepted a scholarship to play for Duke University after his senior season while playing in...
Australia, where he is from! Kyrie's father played professionally there. Kyrie played for the Cleveland Cavaliers from
2011-2017 before heading to Boston and now Brooklyn. Kyrie is an NBA Champion, 6x NBA All-Star, NBA All-Star
Game MVP, USA Basketball Male Athlete of the Year...

Kawhi

2

KAWHI
# LEONARD
F

2018-19 Season Stats

| PPG | RPG | APG | SPG |
|------|------|------|------|
| 26.6 | 7.3 | 3.3 | 1.8 |

| FG% | FT% | 3PT% |
|------|------|------|
| 49.6 | 85.4 | 37.1 |

Kawhi Leonard, born 1991, is currently playing for the NBA in his home town of Los Angeles, California with the LA Clippers. Leonard played college basketball at San Diego state but opted out of his last two seasons to enter the 2011 NBA draft. 2x NBA Champion, 2x NBA Finals MVP, 3x NBA All-Star...

Kemba Walker

### KEMBA
# WALKER
### G

2018-19 Season Stats

| PPG | RPG | APG | SPG |
|------|------|------|------|
| 25.6 | 4.4 | 5.9 | 1.2 |

| FG% | FT% | 3PT% |
|------|------|------|
| 43.4 | 84.4 | 35.6 |

Kemba Walker, born in 1990, is a point guard for the Boston Celtics. Walker grew up in Bronx, New York and played college ball for the Connecticut Huskies. Walker was the nation's second-leading scorer his junior year and also named First Team All-American. Kemba then entered the pros, and became a star in Charlotte prior to going to Boston. 3x NBA All-Star, All-NBA Third Team!

# 34

## GIANNIS
## ANTETOKOUNMPO
### F

2018-19 Season Stats

| PPG | RPG | APG | SPG |
|------|------|------|------|
| 27.7 | 12.5 | 5.9 | 1.3 |

| FG% | FT% | 3PT% |
|------|------|------|
| 57.8 | 72.9 | 25.6 |

Giannis Antetokounmpo was born in 1994 in Athens, Greece. Antetokounmpo began playing basketball while in Athens and became a star, eventually entering the 2013 NBA draft. The next year, he became the first player in NBA history to finish a regular season in the top 20 in total points, rebounds, assists, steals, and blocks. NBA MPV, 3x NBA All-Star, All-NBA First Team... Antetokounmpo rose to fame fast.

Kevin Durant

# 35

2018-19 Season Stats

| PPG | RPG | APG | SPG |
|-----|-----|-----|-----|
| 26.0 | 6.4 | 5.9 | 0.7 |

| FG% | FT% | 3PT% |
|-----|-----|------|
| 52.1 | 88.5 | 35.3 |

Kevin Durant was born in 1988 in Washington, D.C. and played college ball for one year at the University of Texas before being the second overall pick by the Seattle SuperSonics in the 2007 draft. The following year, the Sonics team headed to Oklahoma and then called themselves the Thunder (yeah, the whole thing was wierd). Durant played for OKC for 8 seasons before heading to Golden State. The Warriors had Durant, the 'Splash Brothers' and several other stars, becoming the greatest team in NBA history. 10x All-Star, scoring machine and All-Time Great!

Anthony Davis

ANTHONY
**DAVIS**
PF/C

| PPG | RPG | APG | SPG |
|------|------|------|------|
| 25.9 | 12.0 | 3.9 | 1.6 |

| FG% | FT% | 3PT% |
|------|------|------|
| 51.7 | 79.4 | 33.1 |

Anthony Davis, born 1993, became a superstar playing high school ball growing up in Chicago. Davis played college basketball for Kentucky before he was the 1st overall pick for the New Orleans Hornets. 6x NBA All-Star, NBA All-Star Game MVP, 3x All-NBA First Team, NBA All-Defensive First Team... Many great achievements.

11

Russell Westbrook

# RUSSELL
# WESTBROOK
## PG/G

2018-19 Season Stats

| PPG | RPG | APG | SPG |
|------|------|------|------|
| 22.9 | 11.1 | 10.7 | 1.9 |

| FG% | FT% | 3PT% |
|------|------|------|
| 42.8 | 65.6 | 29.0 |

Russell Westbrook, born 1988, grew up playing basketball. He and his best friend had hopes of playing for UCLA together, until his best friend passed away at a young age. Westbrook decided to carry on his friend's legacy by dedicating himself to the game of basketball. Since, Westbrook has done what no one in basketball believed could ever be accomplished again - to average a triple-double for an entire season. That is, to average 10+ of any three of the following categories: points, rebounds, assists, steals or blocks. Only Oscar Robertson had done this before (50+ years ago) and in 2017, Russell Westbrook did it! The following year... He did it again!! And the year after that? Yep... Did it again!!! Westbrook now plays for the Rockets.

Paul George

13

PAUL
GEORGE
F

2018-19 Season Stats

| PPG | RPG | APG | SPG |
|------|------|------|------|
| 28.0 | 8.2 | 4.1 | 2.2 |

| FG% | FT% | 3PT% |
|------|------|------|
| 43.8 | 83.9 | 38.6 |

Paul George, born in 1990, grew up playing basketball but didn't join a basketball team until high school, where he later became a standout, going on to play for Fresno State. In 2010, George was drafted by the Indiana Pacers. He currently plays in his hometown, Los Angeles, for the LA Clippers. 6x NBA All-Star, All-NBA First Team, 2x NBA All-Defensive First Team, NBA steals leader, No. 24 retired by Fresno State... There's no doubt he's one of the best in the game.

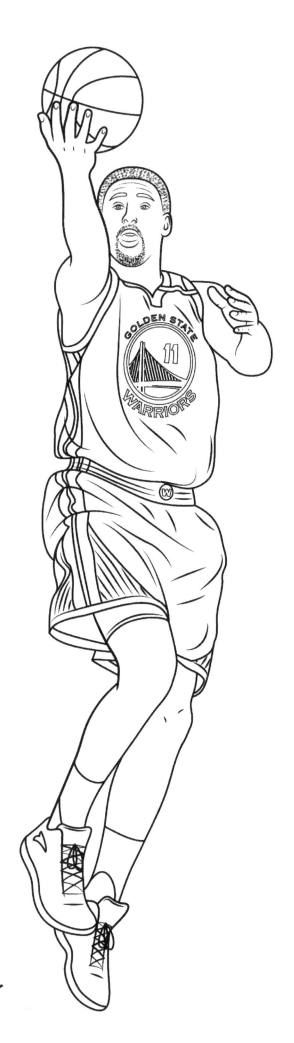

Klay
Thompson

11

2018-19 Season Stats

| PPG | RPG | APG | SPG |
|------|------|------|------|
| 21.5 | 3.8 | 2.4 | 1.1 |

| FG% | FT% | 3PT% |
|------|------|------|
| 46.7 | 81.6 | 40.2 |

Klay Thompson, born in 1990, is one of the standout players on the Golden State Warriors, being credited as one of the greatest shooters in NBA history, behind teammate, Steph Curry. Klay's dad, Michael Thompson, played in the NBA. Klay played college ball for the Washington State Cougars before being selected by the Warriors in 2014. Thompson and Steph Curry set the NBA season record with 484 combined three-pointers, earthing them the nickname the "Splash Brothers." 3x NBA champion, 5x NBA All-Star, 2x All-NBA Third Team...

# 32

## KARL-ANTHONY
## TOWNS
### C

MINNESOTA

32

MINNESOTA TIMBERWOLVES

2018-19 Season Stats

| PPG | RPG | APG | SPG |
|------|------|-----|-----|
| 24.4 | 12.4 | 3.4 | 0.9 |

| FG% | FT% | 3PT% |
|------|------|------|
| 51.8 | 83.6 | 40.0 |

Karl-Anthony Towns, born in 1995, is a Dominican-American professional basketball player. Towns played college basket-ball at Kentucky before being the number one overall pick in the 2015 NBA Draft by the Minnesota Timberwolves. Towns has remained with the Timberwolves ever since. 2x NBA All-Star, All-NBA Third Team, NBA Rookie of the Year...

Blake Griffin

# 23

## BLAKE GRIFFIN
### F

DETROIT PISTONS

**2018-19 Season Stats**

| PPG | RPG | APG | SPG |
|------|------|------|------|
| 24.9 | 7.5 | 5.4 | 0.7 |

| FG% | FT% | 3PT% |
|------|------|------|
| 46.2 | 75.3 | 36.2 |

Blake Griffin was born in 1989 in Oklahoma City, Ok. His high school won the state title every year he attended, 4 straight! Despite this, Griffin hardly was recruited, except by in-state, University of Oklahoma. Griffin committed and played two college basketball seasons as a Sooner before being selected in the 2009 NBA Draft by the Clippers. In 2018, he was traded to Detroit. 6x NBA All-Star, 3x All-NBA Second Team, NBA Rookie of the Year, NBA Slam Dunk Contest Champion and No. 23 retired by Oklahoma. Thanks to nearly a 40" vertical, Griffin is one of the most explosive dunkers the NBA has ever seen!

Damian
Lillard

0

2018-19 Season Stats

| PPG | RPG | APG | SPG |
|------|------|-----|-----|
| 25.8 | 4.6 | 6.9 | 1.1 |

| FG% | FT% | 3PT% |
|------|------|------|
| 44.4 | 91.2 | 36.9 |

Damian Lillard (b. 1990) grew up in Oakland, California. He has spent his entire 7-season NBA career with the Portland Trailblazers. After a solid high school career, Lillard accepted a scholarship to play for Weber State in Utah. The Trailblazers selected him 6th overall in the 2012 NBA draft!  4x NBA All-Star, All-NBA First and Third Teams, NBA Rookie of the Year...

Luka Dončić

**77**

# Luka
# DONČIĆ
## G/SF

2018-19 Season Stats

| PPG | RPG | APG | SPG |
| --- | --- | --- | --- |
| 21.2 | 7.8 | 6.0 | 1.1 |

| FG% | FT% | 3PT% |
| --- | --- | --- |
| 42.7 | 71.3 | 32.7 |

Luka Doncic (b. 1999) grew up in Ljubljana, Slovenia and is a 6'7" 'point forward', and brings an entirely new creative style to the NBA. Third overall pick in the 2018 NBA Draft, after an insanely successful overseas career, Luka has set the NBA on fire in just a season and a half. In just his second season, he averaged nearly a triple double, close to 30 points per game average and named a starter in the 2020 NBA All-Star Game. No one has started like this besides a select few...

Kevin Love

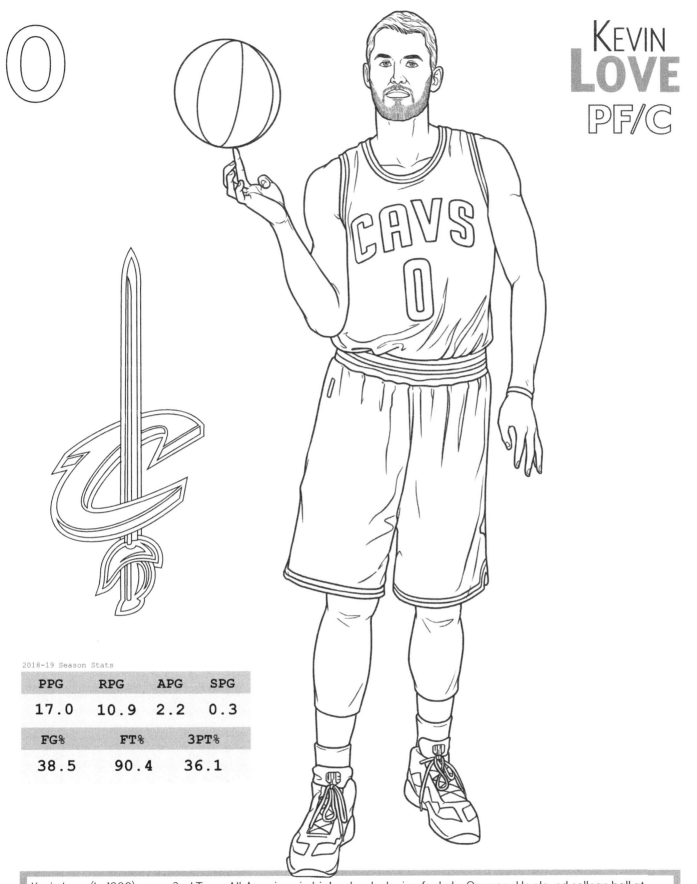

# O

**2018-19 Season Stats**

| PPG | RPG | APG | SPG |
|------|------|-----|-----|
| 17.0 | 10.9 | 2.2 | 0.3 |

| FG% | FT% | 3PT% |
|------|------|------|
| 38.5 | 90.4 | 36.1 |

Kevin Love (b. 1988) was a 2nd-Team All-American in high school, playing for Lake Oswego. He played college ball at UCLA, where as a freshman, he earned 1st-Team All-American honors and led the Bruin's to the Final Four. 4th overall pick in the 2008 NBA Draft. Has since won an NBA Championship with LeBron in 2016, voted 5x an NBA All-Star, 2x All-NBA 2nd Team, NBA 3-point contest winner, and also earned the NBA's Most Improved Player of the Year Award!

Donovan Mitchell

Rudy Gobert

# 27

## RUDY GOBERT
C

**2018-2019 Regular Season Stats**

| PPG | RPG | APG | SPG |
|------|------|------|------|
| 15.9 | 12.9 | 2.0 | 0.8 |

| FG% | FT% | 3PT% |
|------|------|------|
| 66.9 | 63.6 | – |

Rudy Gobert (b. 1992) who's full French last name is Gobert-Bourgarel is an absolute defensive machine, intimidating opposing teams with his 7'9" wingspan and 7'1" height. Gobert was raised in Aisne, which is north of France and very quickly had success playing in the French leagues. The 27th overall pick in the 2013 NBA Draft, Rudy has since earned 3x NBA All-D team awards, All-NBA 2nd and 3rd team selections and won back-to-back NBA Defensive POY honors!

Ben Simmons

# BEN
# SIMMONS

G

25

| 2018-2019 Regular Season Stats | | | |
|---|---|---|---|
| PPG | RPG | APG | SPG |
| 16.9 | 8.8 | 7.7 | 1.4 |
| FG% | FT% | 3PT% | |
| 56.3 | 60.0 | 0.0 | |

Victor Oladipo

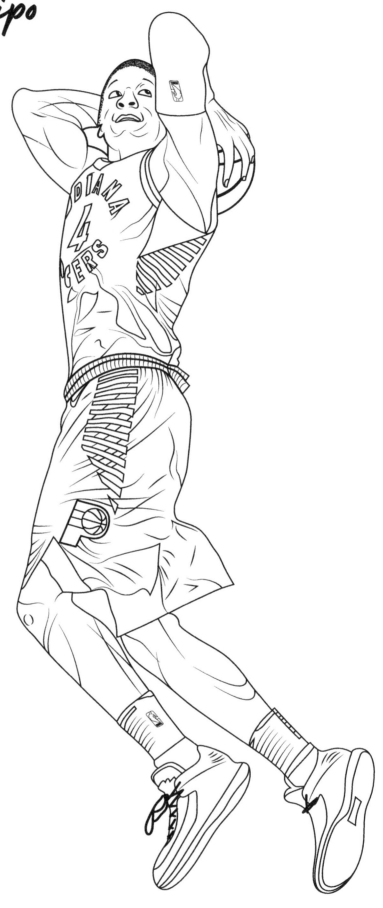

VICTOR
**OLADIPO**
4 G

Pacers

2018-2019 Regular Season Stats

| PPG | RPG | APG | SPG |
| --- | --- | --- | --- |
| 18.8 | 5.6 | 5.2 | 1.7 |

| FG% | FT% | 3PT% |
| --- | --- | --- |
| 42.3 | 73.0 | 34.3 |

22

Jimmy Butler

# JIMMY BUTLER

G

## Miami 22

| 2018-2019 Regular Season Stats | | | |
|---|---|---|---|
| PPG | RPG | APG | SPG |
| 18.7 | 5.3 | 4.0 | 1.9 |
| FG% | | FT% | 3PT% |
| 46.2 | | 85.5 | 34.7 |

23

DeMar DeRozan

DeMar
**DeRozan**

G

10

2018-19 Season Stats

| PPG | RPG | APG | SPG |
|------|------|------|------|
| 21.2 | 6.0 | 6.2 | 1.1 |

| FG% | FT% | 3PT% |
|------|------|------|
| 48.1 | 83.0 | 15.6 |

Zion Williamson

ZION
**WILLIAMSON**
F

NEW ORLEANS
PELICANS

22 Games into 2019-20 Season.

| PPG | RPG | APG | SPG |
|------|------|------|------|
| 22.3 | 6.4 | 2.1 | 0.7 |

| FG% | FT% | 3PT% |
|------|------|------|
| 57.9 | 63.6 | 42.9 |

25

NIKOLA
JOKIĆ
C

15

DENVER
15

DENVER
NUGGETS

Nikola Jokic aka the 'Joker' aka 'Big Honey' (yep that's one of his nicknames) was born and raised in Serbia and despite being 7 feet tall, he hit the ground running in terms of playing ability. An excellent passer, and overall playmaker. Following thre 2018-19 season, Nikola was named All-NBA 1st Team, aka 'the best Center in the NBA!'

2018-19 Season Stats

| PPG | RPG | APG | SPG |
|------|-------|------|------|
| 20.1 | 10.8 | 7.3 | 1.4 |

| FG% | FT% | 3PT% |
|------|------|------|
| 51.1 | 82.1 | 30.7 |

# NBA 2021 ALL★STAR RESERVES

MARC
GASOL
C

33

2018-2019 Regular Season Stats

| PPG | RPG | APG | SPG |
|------|------|------|------|
| 13.6 | 7.9 | 4.4 | 1.1 |

| FG% | FT% | 3PT% |
|------|------|------|
| 44.8 | 75.9 | 36.3 |

TORONTO RAPTORS

PAUL
# MILLSAP
## PF

4

2018-2019 Regular Season Stats

| PPG | RPG | APG | SPG |
|------|------|------|------|
| 12.6 | 7.2 | 2.0 | 1.2 |

| FG% | FT% | 3PT% |
|------|------|------|
| 48.4 | 72.7 | 36.5 |

KHRIS
**MIDDLETON**
G/F 22

2018-19 Season Stats

| PPG | RPG | APG | SPG |
|------|------|------|------|
| 18.3 | 6.0 | 4.3 | 1.0 |

| FG% | FT% | 3PT% |
|------|------|------|
| 44.1 | 83.7 | 37.8 |

# GORDON HAYWARD

F

20

2018-2019 Regular Season Stats

| PPG | RPG | APG | SPG |
|------|------|------|------|
| 11.5 | 4.5 | 3.4 | 0.9 |

| FG% | FT% | 3PT% |
|------|------|------|
| 46.6 | 83.4 | 33.3 |

MALCOLM
**BROGDON**
G

| 2018-2019 Regular Season Stats | | | |
|---|---|---|---|
| PPG | RPG | APG | SPG |
| 15.6 | 4.5 | 3.2 | 0.9 |
| FG% | FT% | 3PT% | |
| 50.5 | 92.8 | 42.6 | |

GORAN
**DRAGIC**

G

7

2018-2019 Regular Season Stats

| PPG | RPG | APG | SPG |
|------|------|------|------|
| 13.7 | 3.1 | 4.8 | 0.8 |

| FG% | FT% | 3PT% |
|------|------|------|
| 41.3 | 78.2 | 34.8 |

29

R.J.
**BARRETT**
G

as of 56 games into 2019-20 season.

| PPG | RPG | APG | SPG |
|------|------|------|------|
| 14.3 | 5.0 | 2.6 | 1.0 |

| FG% | FT% | 3PT% |
|------|------|------|
| 40.2 | 61.4 | 32.0 |

# 12

## LaMarcus ALDRIDGE
### F

| 2018-19 Season Stats | | | |
| PPG | RPG | APG | SPG |
| --- | --- | --- | --- |
| 21.3 | 9.2 | 2.4 | 0.5 |
| FG% | FT% | 3PT% | |
| 51.9 | 84.7 | 23.8 | |

SAN ANTONIO SPURS

# 3

ANDRE
**DRUMMOND**
©

2018-2019 Regular Season Stats

| PPG | RPG | APG | SPG |
|------|------|------|------|
| 17.3 | 15.6 | 1.4 | 1.7 |

| FG% | FT% | 3PT% |
|------|------|------|
| 53.3 | 59.0 | 13.2 |

# NIKOLA
# VUČEVIĆ
C

9

2018-19 Season Stats

| PPG | RPG | APG | SPG |
|-----|-----|-----|-----|
| 20.8 | 12.0 | 3.8 | 1.0 |

| FG% | | FT% | | 3PT% |
|-----|---|-----|---|------|
| 51.8 | | 78.9 | | 36.4 |

6

KRISTAPS
**PORZINGIS**
G

NEW YORK KNICKS

2017-2018 Regular Season Stats

| PPG | RPG | APG | SPG |
|------|------|------|------|
| 22.7 | 6.6 | 1.2 | 0.8 |
| **FG%** | **FT%** | **3PT%** | |
| 43.8 | 79.3 | 39.3 | |

DEVIN
**BOOKER**
G

2018-2019 Regular Season Stats

| PPG | RPG | APG | SPG |
|------|------|------|------|
| 26.6 | 4.1 | 6.8 | 0.9 |

| FG% | FT% | 3PT% |
|------|------|------|
| 46.7 | 86.6 | 32.6 |

**32**

2

JOHN
**WALL**
PG

2018-2019 Regular Season Stats

| PPG | RPG | APG | SPG |
|------|------|------|------|
| 20.7 | 3.6 | 8.7 | 1.5 |

| FG% | FT% | 3PT% |
|------|------|------|
| 42.0 | 69.7 | 30.2 |

# AL **HORFORD**

## PF

2017-2018 Regular Season Stats

| PPG | RPG | APG | SPG |
|-----|-----|-----|-----|
| 12.9 | 7.4 | 4.7 | 0.6 |

| FG% | FT% | 3PT% |
|-----|-----|------|
| 48.9 | 78.3 | 42.9 |

# 42

DeAndre
JORDAN
©

6

JORDAN
6

2018-2019 Regular Season Stats

| PPG | RPG | APG | SPG |
|------|------|------|------|
| 11.0 | 13.1 | 2.3 | 0.6 |
| FG% | FT% | 3PT% | |
| 64.5 | 58.0 | 0.00 | |

NETS

DE'AARON
FOX PG

2018-2019 Regular Season Stats

| PPG | RPG | APG | SPG |
|------|------|------|------|
| 17.3 | 3.8 | 7.3 | 1.6 |

| FG% | FT% | 3PT% |
|------|------|------|
| 45.8 | 72.7 | 37.1 |

# D'Angelo
# RUSSELL
PG
1

MINNESOTA
TIMBERWOLVES

2018-2019 Regular Season Stats

| PPG | RPG | APG | SPG |
|------|------|------|------|
| 21.1 | 3.9 | 7.0 | 1.2 |

| FG% | FT% | 3PT% |
|------|------|------|
| 43.4 | 78.0 | 36.9 |

NOTE:
Player's jersey does not
reflect his current team.

**24**

LAURI
**MARKKANEN**
PF

CHICAGO
BULLS

2018-2019 Regular Season Stats

| PPG | RPG | APG | SPG |
|------|------|------|------|
| 18.7 | 9.0 | 1.4 | 0.7 |

| FG% | FT% | 3PT% |
|------|------|------|
| 43.0 | 87.2 | 36.1 |

35

BRANDON
**INGRAM**
F

14

NEW ORLEANS
PELICANS

2018-2019 Regular Season Stats

| PPG | RPG | APG | SPG |
|------|------|------|------|
| 18.3 | 5.1 | 3.0 | 0.5 |

| FG% | FT% | 3PT% |
|------|------|------|
| 49.7 | 67.5 | 33.0 |

# HASSAN
# WHITESIDE
## C

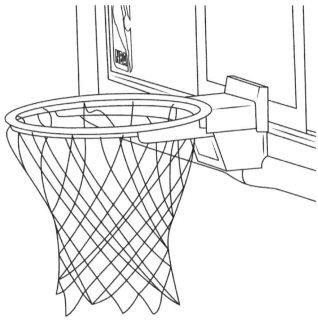

| PPG | RPG | APG | SPG |
|------|------|------|------|
| 12.3 | 11.3 | 0.8 | 0.6 |

| FG% | | FT% | | 3PT% |
|------|------|------|------|------|
| 57.1 | | 44.9 | | 12.5 |

21

PASCAL
SIAKAM
PF
43

| PPG | RPG | APG | SPG |
|------|------|------|------|
| 16.9 | 6.9 | 3.1 | 0.9 |

| FG% | FT% | 3PT% |
|------|------|------|
| 54.9 | 78.5 | 36.9 |

7

KYLE
LOWRY
G

2018-2019 Regular Season Stats

| PPG | RPG | APG | SPG |
|------|------|------|------|
| 14.2 | 4.8 | 8.7 | 1.4 |

| FG% | FT% | 3PT% |
|------|------|------|
| 41.1 | 83.0 | 34.7 |

3

BRADLEY
**BEAL**
G

2018-2019 Regular Season Stats

| PPG | RPG | APG | SPG |
|------|------|------|------|
| 25.6 | 5.0 | 5.5 | 1.5 |

| FG% | FT% | 3PT% |
|------|------|------|
| 47.5 | 80.8 | 35.1 |

# SLAM DUNK
## CONTEST

ABOVE THE rim

2015
**SLAM DUNK** CONTEST WINNER
2016

ZACH LAVINE

44.0"

ABOVE THE rim

ABOVE THE rim

DWIGHT HOWARD

NBA RECORD

Reached 12'6" height!
That is 30" above the rim!

2008 SLAM DUNK CONTEST WINNER

39.5"

YOU ARE REQUIRED TO TURN BOOK SIDEWAYS TO COLOR.. YOU MUST. It is the law.

39

NATE ROBINSON

ABOVE THE rim

43.5"

NBA RECORD
Most all-time contest wins.
2006, 2009 and 2010!

3 TIMES
SLAM DUNK CONTEST WINNER

40

ABOVE THE rim

40.5"

DONOVAN MITCHELL

2018
SLAM DUNK CONTEST WINNER

41

ABOVE THE. rim

MICHAEL JORDAN
1987 AND 1988

47.0"

2 TIMES
SLAM DUNK CONTEST WINNER

# JORDAN

**1988 NBA DUNK CONTEST**
Free throw line
180" (15 feet)

47.0"

# TEAM DE IGN

# YOU JUST RECIEVED THIS LETTER IN THE MAIL... YOU ARE AN NBA OWNER!

National Basketball Association
Olympic Tower
645 Fifth Avenue
New York, NY 10022

_____
Date

Ownership Information: Please Print Clearly

_____
Your Name

_____

_____

_____
Mailing address you would like ownership
documents sent to. Please write in above

My name is Adam Silver. I have been the NBA Commissioner since 2014. There have been a few changes during the time I have been the head of this league, but this certainly tops that list and is quite possibly the most exciting news in NBA history!

It hasn't been announced yet but earlier this year we decided it was time to expand and add two new teams. One of these teams was purchased by a recent lottery winner, while the other was unable to sell as quickly. As the season grew closer, the NBA Board of Directors and myself went to the players for help.

The NBA players association held a vote of what they wanted to do with this 'other' team. The results of their vote is why I am writing this letter to you now. The players voted to all pitch in, purchase the second team and then give it away!

Part of the deal was that the winner must be chosen at random so we compiled every address listed in the United States, had an automated drawing and this letter was then mailed out to the new owner.

That owner is you!  Congratulations!

Sincerely,

Adam Silver
NBA Commissioner

## BUT BEFORE YOU CAN DRAFT PLAYERS, BUILD A STADIUM OR PLAY A GAME...

## YOU NEED TO CREATE YOUR TEAM!

## REGISTRATION FORM

_____    _____    _____
Owner name                          Age           Hometown

Team will be located in: _____    _____
                              City             State

┌                    ┐          ┌──────────────────────────┐
                                │                          │
                                │  _____       │
└                    ┘          │      Team name           │
   Official use only            └──────────────────────────┘


                                 _____
                                        Mascot

Running an NBA team is no different than running a business. Once team is setup and assembled. You will need a President and also a players agent. Please list names below and reason for selection.

| NAME | REASON FOR SELECTION |
|------|----------------------|
| _____ President _____ | _____ |
| _____ Players agent _____ | _____ |

_____
Owner signature

## CREATE YOUR TEAM LOGO

FORMAT 1                 MAIN LOGO

THIS IS YOUR PRIMARY LOGO - INCLUDE LOGO, CITY NAME AND TEAM NAME

FORMAT 2         ICON LOGO

SIMPLE VERSION (LESS DETAIL. NO CITY/TEAM INFO)

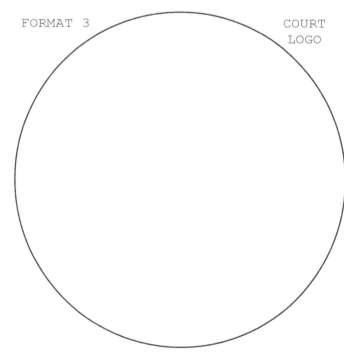

FORMAT 3            COURT LOGO

COURT VERSION (CENTER CIRCLE ON BASKETBALL COURT)

# CREATE YOUR JERSEY
HOME TEAM VERSION

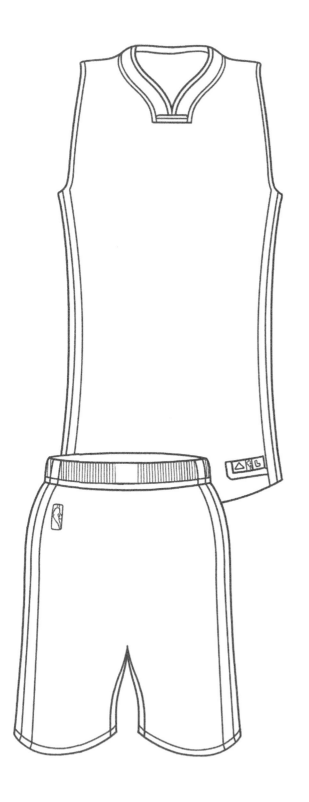

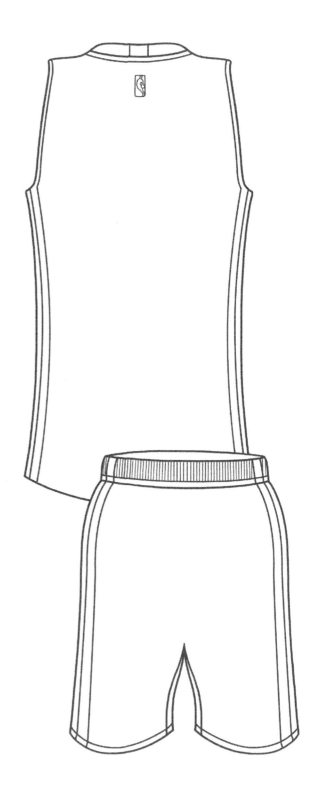

# CREATE YOUR JERSEY
AWAY TEAM VERSION

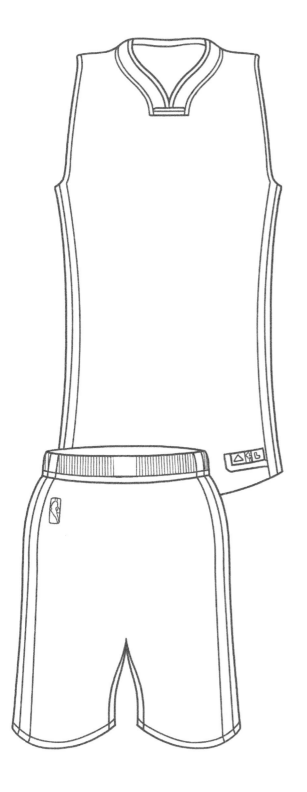

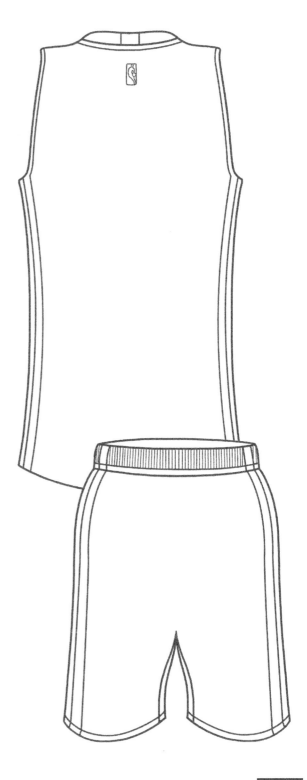

PLAYER JERSEY NUMBER

# 

## PLAYER CARD

Personal

_____
Player name

_____   _____   _____
Position      Height       Weight

_____       _____
College            Hometown

College Statistics

_____   _____   _____
PPG           RPG           APG

_____   _____   _____
SPG           BPG           FG%

PPG    points per game (average)      SPG    steals per game (average)
RPG    rebounds per game (average)    BPG    blocks per game (average)
APG    assists per game (average)     FG%    field goal (shots) percentage

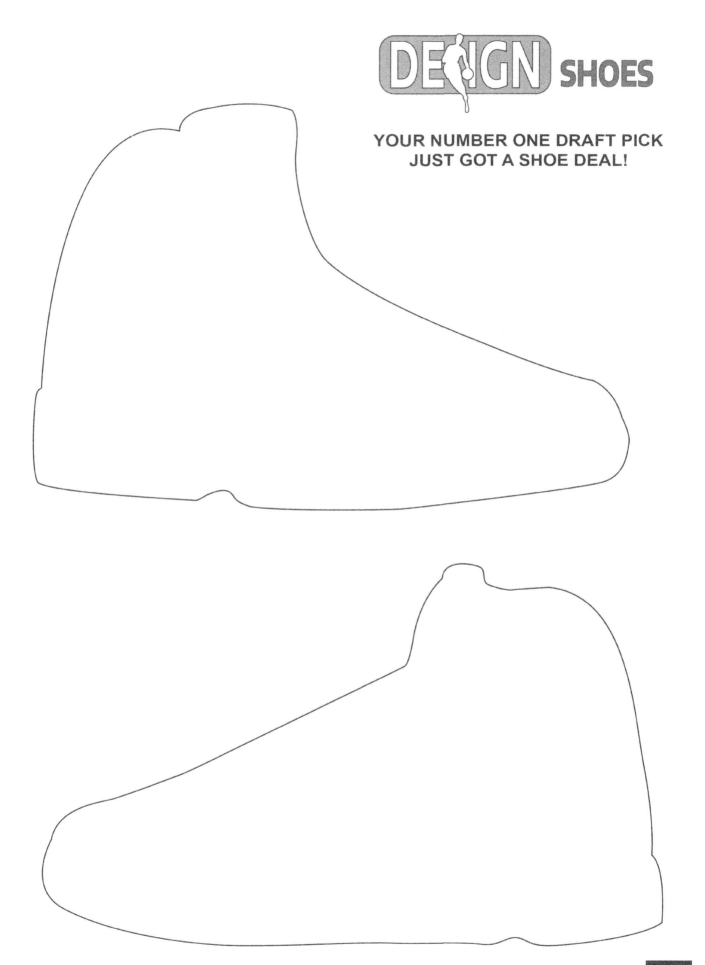

**DESIGN** SHOES

YOUR NUMBER ONE DRAFT PICK
JUST GOT A SHOE DEAL!

47

## Create your team's motion* offense

*A motion offense is one that is always moving. Players pass the ball, screen and move to different spots on the court, typically into another players position and eventually will return to their starting location.

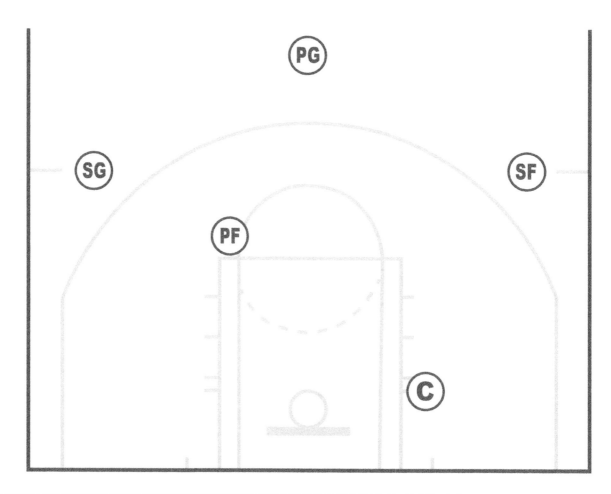

| POSITION | Position # ABBREVIATION | Role | Player Traits | Greats at the POSITION |
|---|---|---|---|---|
| Point Guard | PG¹ | The 'Quarterback' of the team. Primary role is to bring up ball, run offense and find open players. | Excellent ball handling skills. Court vision. Usually best passer, helping others score. | Magic Johnson Stephen Curry |
| Shooting Guard | SG² | Typically primary scorer on team and good outside shooter. Also helps bring ball up court. Well rounded position. | Great shooter, good ball handler. Can take 3-pointer or drive to the hoop. | Michael Jordan Kobe Bryant |
| Small Forward | SF³ | Usually the most versatile player on both ends of the court, able to play and cover the opposing teams center as well as their guards. | Mix of skills. Able to effectively dribble, pass and shoot. | LeBron James Larry Bird |
| Power Forward | PF⁴ | Shares majority of rebounding and inside defensive responsibility with center position. Must be strong but also quick. | Tall and most likely to be strongest player on floor. Great rebounder. Inside shooter. | Kevin Garnett Karl Malone |
| Center | C⁵ | Almost always the tallest player on the team. Shot blocking, rebounding, put-backs and assortment of close range shots. 'Foundation' of team. | Tallest player in lineup. Stays down low near the hoop. Great rebounder, short range shooter. | Shaquille O'neal Wilt Chamberlain |

## EXAMPLE

4.9 seconds left. Down by 2. Your ball. Inbound location marked with → ⒝ . Defenders setup in positions marked→ X .
You have 5 players (mark as→ ○ ). One (1) must throw in ball.
Each player only has time to perform one (1) action.
Actions listed/marked below:

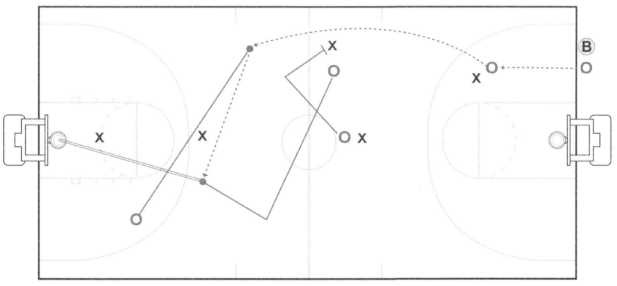

---

## SCENERIO 1

5.8 seconds left. Down by 1. Your ball. Inbound location marked with → ⒝ . Defenders setup in positions marked→ X .
You have 5 players (mark as→ ○ ). One (1) must throw in ball.
Each player only has time to perform one (1) action.
Actions listed/marked below, good luck!

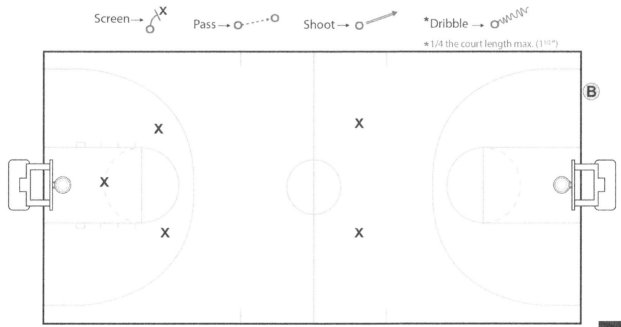

### SCENERIO 2

2.7 seconds left. Tie game. Your ball. Inbound location marked with → Ⓑ. Defenders setup in positions marked → **X**.
You have 5 players (<u>marked</u> as → **O**). One (1) passes in ball.
Two (2) players can screen, one (1) can pass and another (1) can shoot. Actions listed/marked below:

Screen → ⟋ **X**     Pass → O------•O     Shoot → O ↗

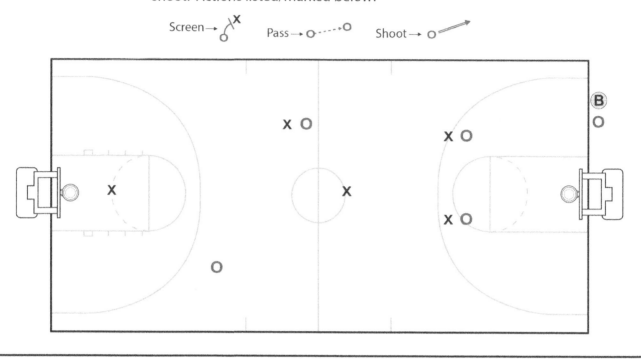

---

### SCENERIO 3

10.1 seconds left. Down by 1. Your ball. Inbound location marked with → Ⓑ. Defenders setup in positions marked → **X**.
You have 5 players (<u>marked</u> as → **O**). One (1) passes in ball.
Two (2) players can screen, one (1) can dribble and pass and another (1) can shoot. Actions listed/marked below:

Screen → ⟋ **X**     Pass → O------•O     Shoot → O ↗     *Dribble → O∿∿∿

*1/4 the court length max. (1½")

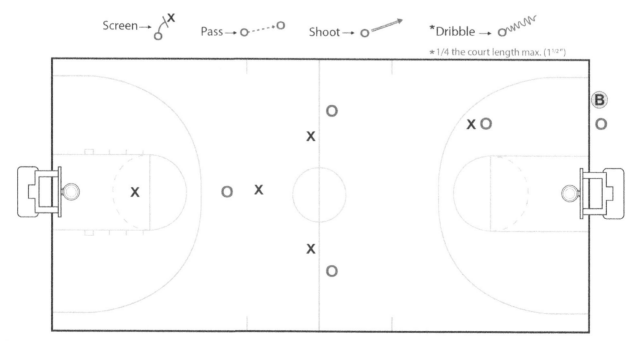

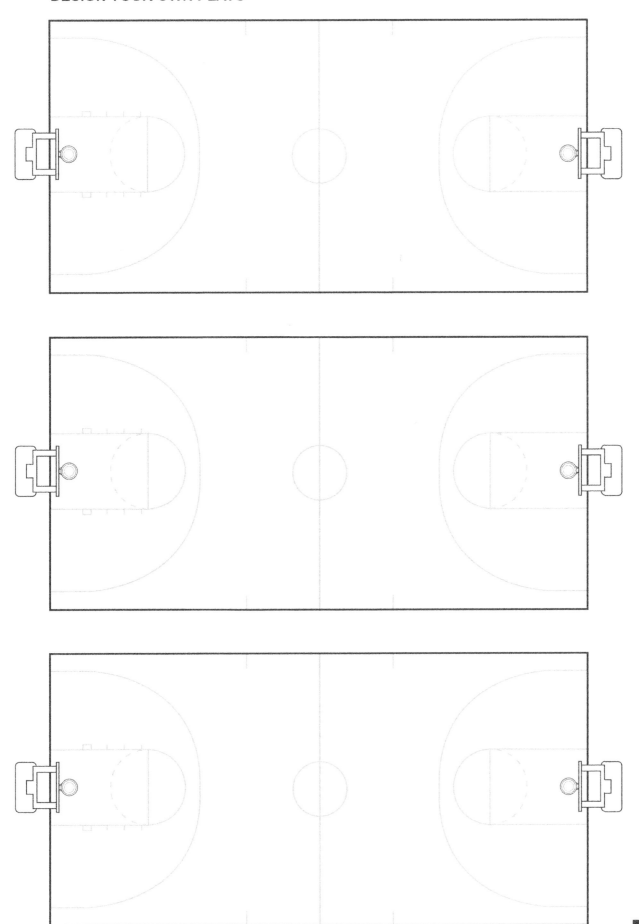

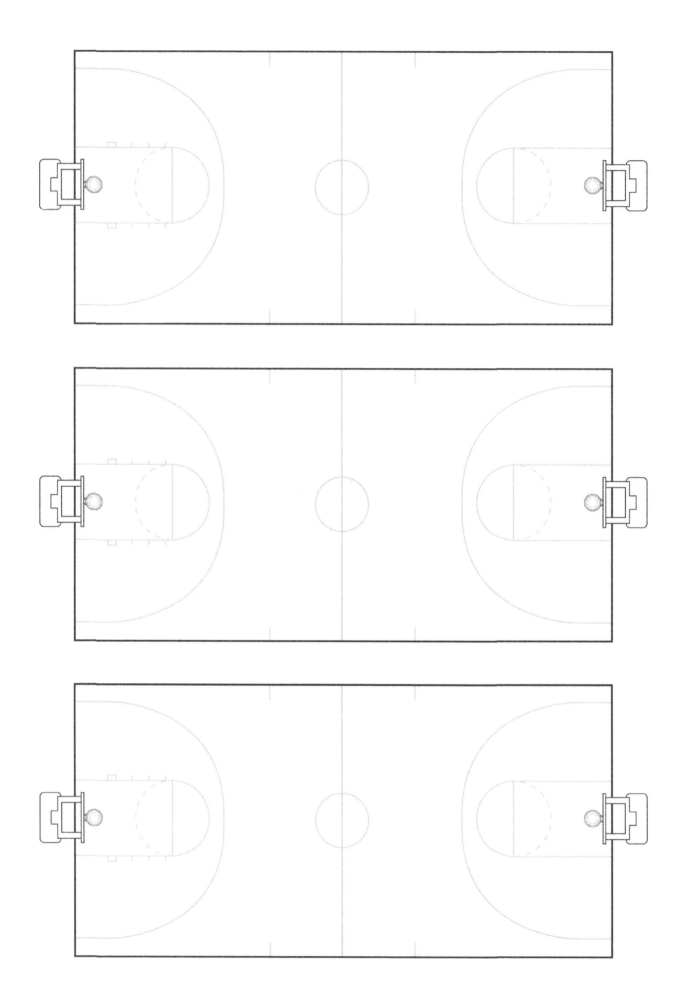

**You've been asked to design the next Air Jordan shoe!**

J O R D A N

NIKE

The new Air Jordan _____ #

" _____

The nickname you are giving these Jordan's

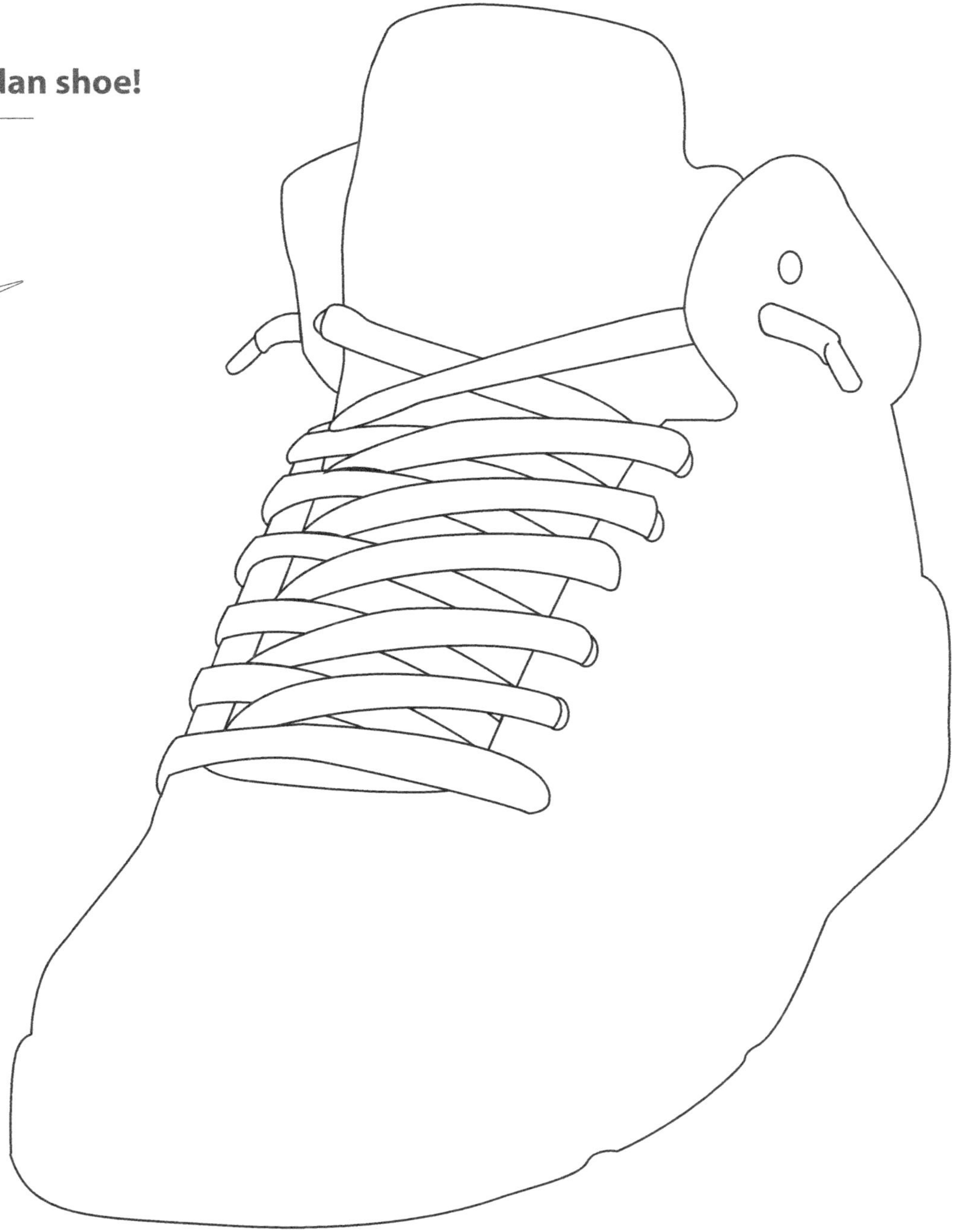

Designed by _____

If you enjoy designing and creating your own Air Jordan's, check out book one in this series: "Retro Air Jordan: Shoes: A Detailed Coloring Book for Adults and Kids" by Anthony Curcio

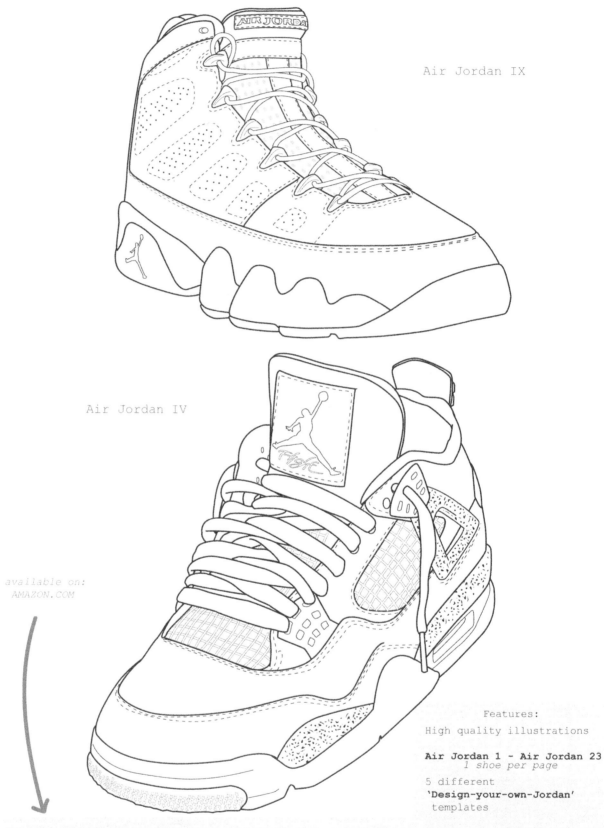

Air Jordan IX

Air Jordan IV

available on:
AMAZON.COM

Features:
High quality illustrations

**Air Jordan 1 - Air Jordan 23**
*1 shoe per page*

5 different
**'Design-your-own-Jordan'**
templates

*"**Retro Air Jordan: Shoes**: A Detailed Coloring Book for Adults and Kids"*
**by Anthony Curcio**

# TEAM Logos

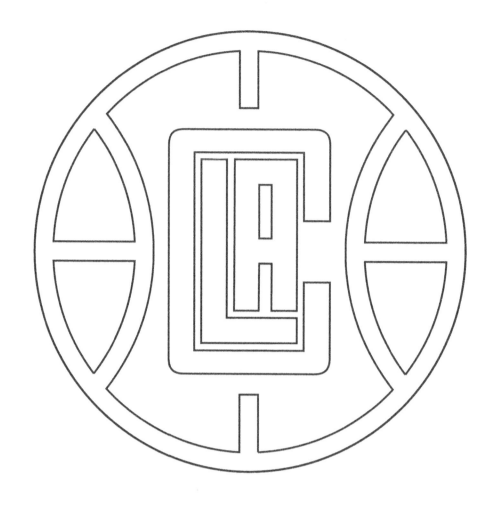

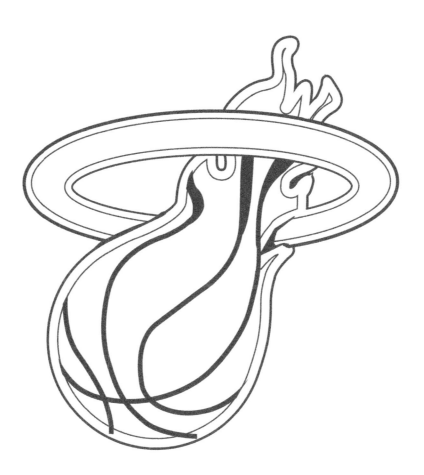

DETROIT PISTONS

GOLDEN STATE WARRIORS

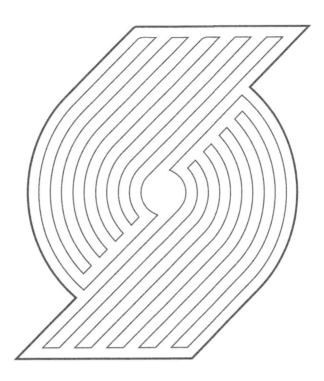

TRAIL BLAZERS

SACRAMENTO
KINGS

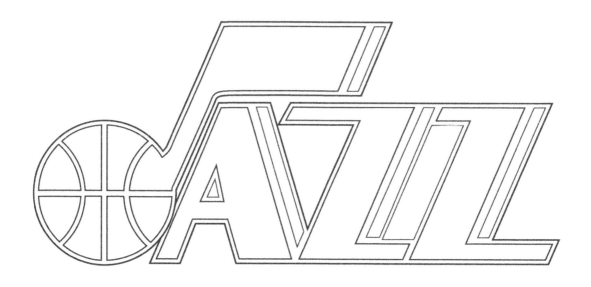

# AIR JORDAN SHOES

During the early 1980's, **Adidas** and **Converse** were the popular shoes to wear on the basketball court.
**Magic Johnson, Larry Bird, Julius Erving,** *all wore Converse.*
**Kareem Abdul Jabbar** and soon **Patrick Ewing** would wear **Addidas.**

Neither Converse **or** Adidas had much interest in signing a young and unproven player named Michael Jordan.

However, Michael Jordan received an offer from a company called **Nike**:

$500,000 a year for five years. Counting stock options, the deal was worth roughly $7 million.
If Jordan brand shoes didn't sell $4 million by the **3**rd year, Nike held the right to cancel the deal.

Before Michael accepted the deal, he approached Adidas - the shoes he preferred at the time - and said:

*"If you guys come anywhere close, I'll sign with you guys."*

Adidas chose to pass on endorsing Michael Jordan, so Michael went with Nike.  The rest, as they say, is history.

Within 2 months of the *Air Jordan 1* being released,
Nike had sold $70 million worth of Air Jordans.

original "Air Jordan" logo

AIR JORDAN 4

The **AIR JORDAN 4**'s have also become one of the most popular Jordan's of all-time based on consumer sales, however this was not always the case. When they first were released in 1989, many people thought they were ugly, but over time they have become legendary...

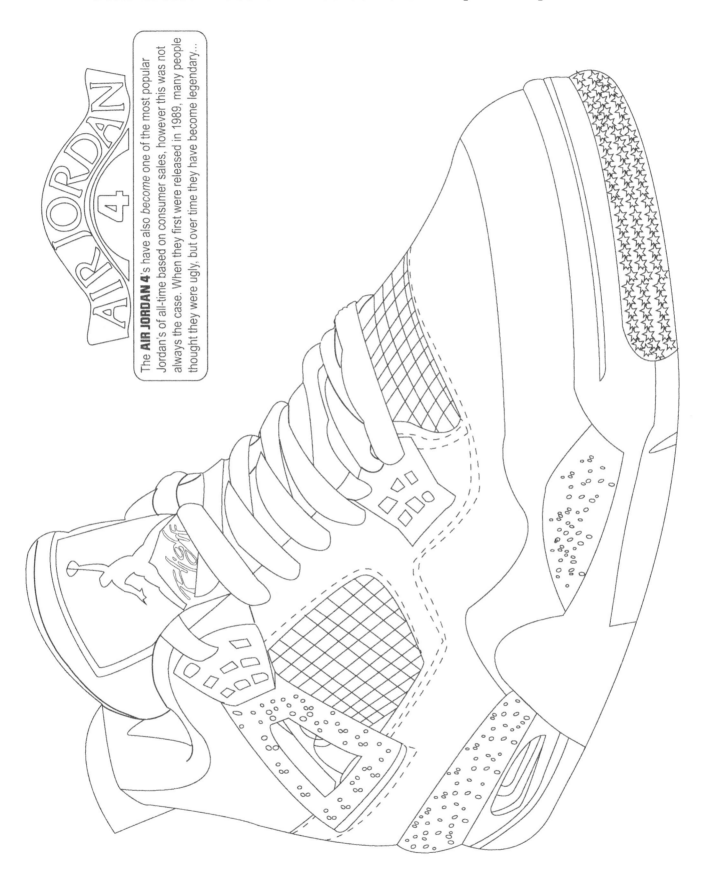

AIR JORDAN 11

The **AIR JORDAN 11** are loved by many sneaker enthusiasts and are always a sell out. Michael was now back in the NBA, and the Air Jordan XI was his shoe. Retailed in 1995 for $124.99 with three different colorways. Arguably the most popular Air Jordan shoe.

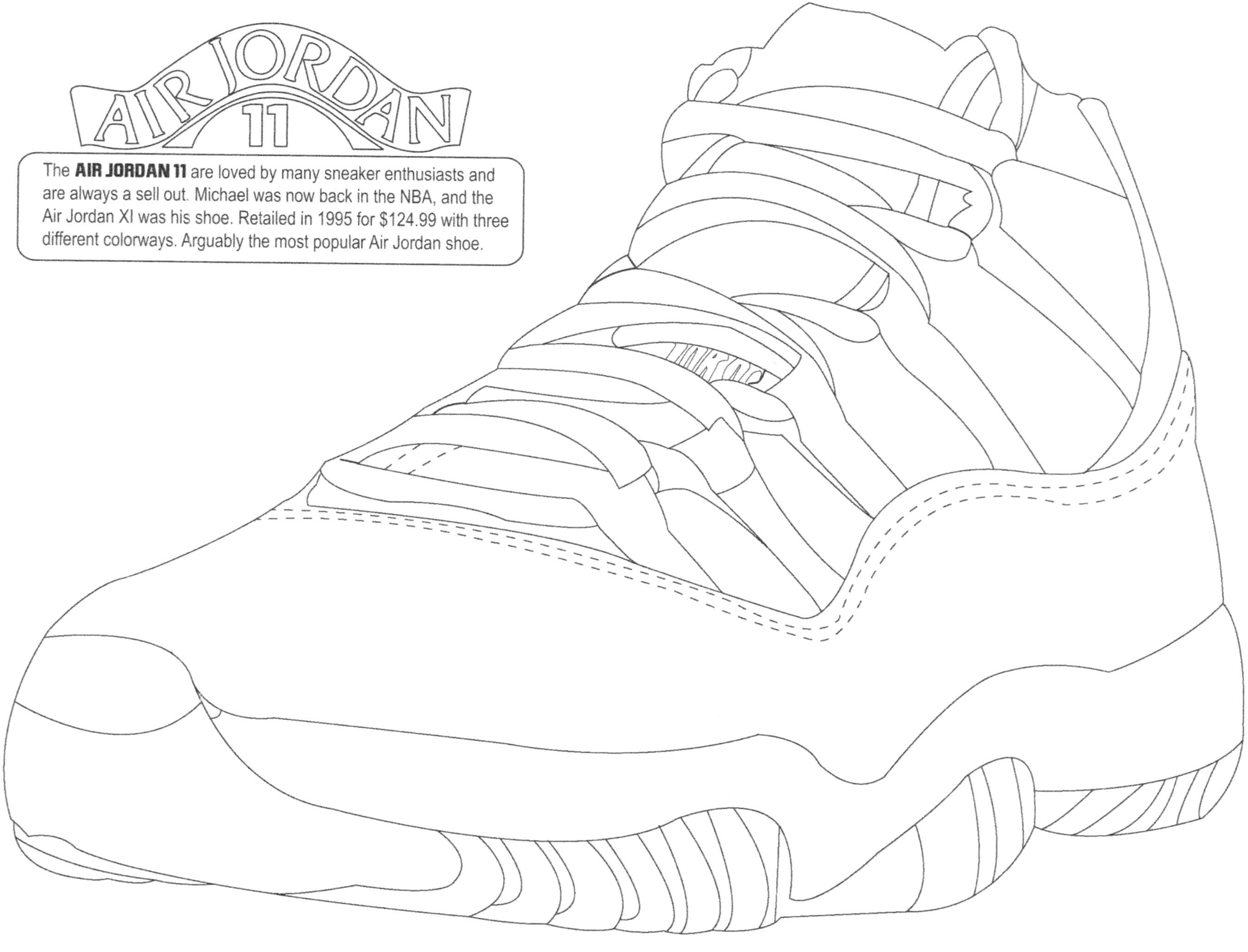

# THE "JUMPMAN" LOGO

**History:**

The famous Air Jordan logo, "Jumpman," was inspired from a *Life Magazine* photoshoot!

**The photo was taken prior to the 1984 Olympics and also before Jordan had ever signed a deal with Nike.**

The photographer, Jacobus Rentmeester (who later sued Nike for unauthorized use), was asking Michael to perform a ballet technique known as a grand jete to add a creative style and give the photo the appearance as if he was going for a dunk.

*The Jordan brand today generates more than $2.5 billion in sales annually, and is projected to generate $4.5 billion a year by 2020.

# THE SHOT ON EHLO

**1989 Eastern Conference First Round
Chicago Bulls vs. Cleveland Cavaliers**

Play By Play:

Michael Jordan hits a jumper with 6 seconds left to give the Bulls a 99-98 lead.

Cleveland calls a timeout.

Craig Ehlo (Cavs) inbounds ball to Larry Nance (Cavs). Nance passes back to Ehlo, who scores on a driving layup giving Cleveland a 100-99 lead with 3 seconds remaining.

Chicago calls a timeout.

Jordan double-teamed by Ehlo and Nance on inbounds. Jordan moves to right, into Ehlo, knocking him off balance, then cut to his left pushing Nance out of way. Brad Sellers (Bulls) passes to Jordan.

Announcer 1:
The inbounds pass comes in to Jordan. Here's Michael at the foul line, the shot on Ehlo... (overlapping Announcer 2) Good! Bulls Win!

Announcer 2:
Good! The Bulls win it! They win it!

# THE BULLS WIN!